All I Want For Christmas Is You

Winter Wonderland

Merry Christmas Everyone

A Holly Jolly Christmas

Do They Know It's Christmas Time

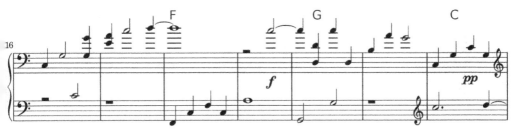
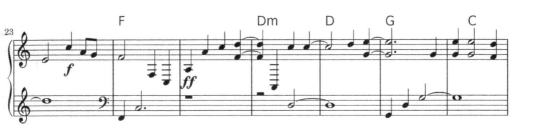

Wonderful Christmastime

The Chipmunk Song

Linus and Lucy

WE THREE KINGS

O Come All Ye Faithful Variation 1

The First Noel Variation 1

The First Noel Variation 2

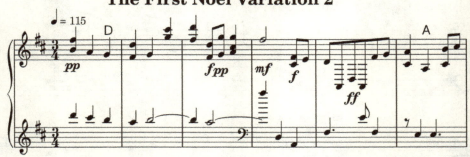

Jingle Bells Variation 1

Jingle Bells Variation 2

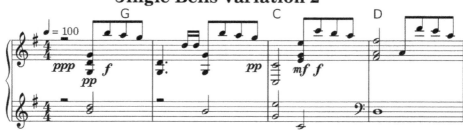

Joy To The World Variation 1

Joy To The World Variation 2

Silent Night variation 1

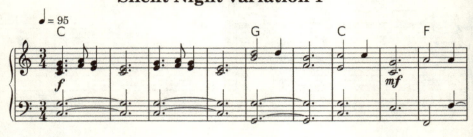

Silent Night Variation 2

O Holy Night Variation 2

O Holy Night Variation 1

Away In A Manger variation 2

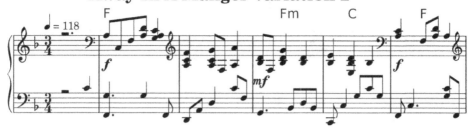

Away In a Manger variation 1

Hark! The Herald Angels Sing variation 2

CAROL OF THE BELLS variation 2

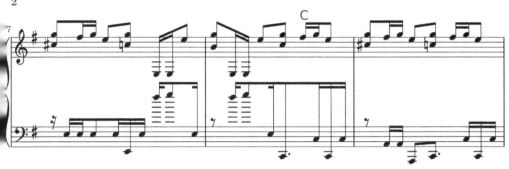
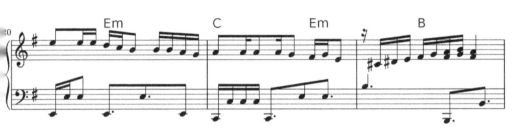
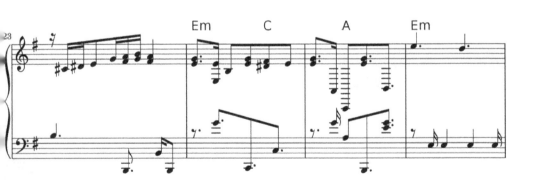

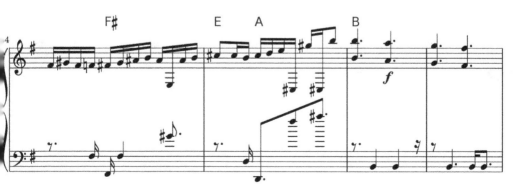

HARK! THE HERALD ANGELS variation 1

CAROL OF THE BELLS variation 1

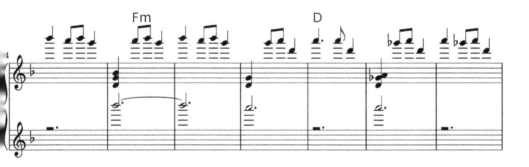

We Wish You a Merry Christmas variation 3

We Wish You A Merry Christmas Variation 2

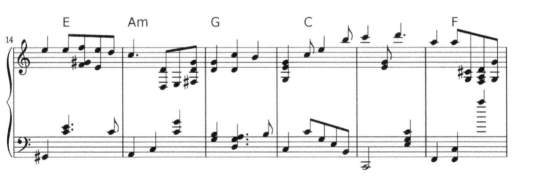
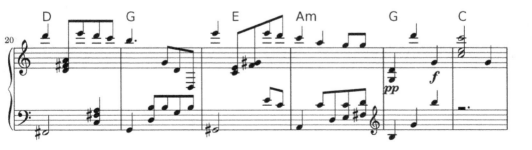

We Wish You A Merry Christmas variation 1

Printed in the USA
CPSIA information can be obtained
at www.ICGtesting.com
LVHW092311051224
798471LV00033B/824